As of May 17, 2012, this guidance applies to federal savings associations in addition to national banks.*

A-RCR

Comptroller of the Currency
Administrator of National Banks

I0439146

Rating Credit Risk

Comptroller's Handbook

April 2001

Rating Credit Risk   Table of Contents

Introduction

Credit risk is the primary financial risk in the banking system and exists in virtually all income-producing activities. How a bank selects and manages its credit risk is critically important to its performance over time; indeed, capital depletion through loan losses has been the proximate cause of most institution failures. Identifying and rating credit risk is the essential first step in managing it effectively.

The OCC expects national banks to have credit risk management systems that produce accurate and timely risk ratings. Likewise, the OCC considers accurate classification of credit among its top supervisory priorities. This booklet describes the elements of an effective internal process for rating credit risk. It also provides guidance on regulatory classifications supplemental to that found in other OCC credit-related booklets, and should be consulted whenever a credit-related examination is conducted.

This handbook provides a comprehensive, but generic, discussion of the objectives and general characteristics of effective credit risk rating systems. In practice, a bank's risk rating system should reflect the complexity of its lending activities and the overall level of risk involved. No single credit risk rating system is ideal for every bank. Large banks typically require sophisticated rating systems involving multiple rating grades. On the other hand, community banks that lend primarily within their geographic area will typically be able to adhere to this guidance in a less formal and systematic manner because of the simplicity of their credit exposures and management's direct knowledge of customers' credit needs and financial conditions.

Functions of a Credit Risk Rating System

Well-managed credit risk rating systems promote bank safety and soundness by facilitating informed decision making. Rating systems measure credit risk and differentiate individual credits and groups of credits by the risk they pose. This allows bank management and examiners to monitor changes and trends in risk levels. The process also allows bank management to manage risk to optimize returns.

Credit risk ratings are also essential to other important functions, such as:

- Credit approval and underwriting C Risk ratings should be used to determine or influence who is authorized to approve a credit, how much credit will be extended or held, and the structure of the credit facility (collateral, repayment terms, guarantor, etc.).

- Loan pricing C Risk ratings should guide price setting. The price for taking credit risk must be sufficient to compensate for the risk to earnings and capital. Incorrect pricing can lead to risk/return imbalances, lost business, and adverse selection.[1]

- Relationship management and credit administration C A credit's risk rating should determine how the relationship is administered. Higher risk credits should be reviewed and analyzed more frequently, and higher risk borrowers normally should be contacted more frequently. Problem and marginal relationships generally require intensive supervision by management and problem loan/workout specialists.

- Allowance for loan and lease losses (ALLL) and capital adequacy C Risk ratings of individual credits underpin the ALLL. Every credit's inherent loss should be factored into its assigned risk rating with an allowance provided either individually or on a pooled basis. The ALLL must be directly correlated with the level of risk indicated by risk ratings. Ratings are also useful in determining the appropriate amount of capital to absorb extraordinary, unexpected credit losses.

- Portfolio management information systems (MIS) and board reporting C Risk rating reports that aggregate and stratify risk and describe risk's trends within the portfolio are critical to credit risk management and strategic decision making.

- Traditional and advanced portfolio management C Risk ratings strongly influence banks' decisions to buy, sell, hold, and hedge credit facilities.

---

[1] Adverse selection occurs when pricing or other underwriting and marketing factors cause too few desirable risk prospects relative to undesirable risk prospects to respond to a credit offering.

Expectations of Bank Credit Risk Rating Systems

No single credit risk rating system is ideal for every bank. The attributes described below should be present in all systems, but how banks combine those attributes to form a process will vary. The OCC expects the following of a national bank's risk rating system:

- The system should be integrated into the bank's overall portfolio risk management. It should form the foundation for credit risk measurement, monitoring, and reporting, and it should support management's and the board's decision making.

- The board of directors should approve the credit risk rating system and assign clear responsibility and accountability for the risk rating process. The board should receive sufficient information to oversee management's implementation of the process.

- All credit exposures should be rated. (Where individual credit risk ratings are not assigned, e.g., small-denomination performing loans, banks should assign the portfolio of such exposures a composite credit risk rating that adequately defines its risk, i.e., repayment capacity and loss potential.)

- The risk rating system should assign an adequate number of ratings. To ensure that risks among pass credits (i.e., those that are not adversely rated) are adequately differentiated, most rating systems require several pass grades.

- Risk ratings must be accurate and timely.

- The criteria for assigning each rating should be clear and precisely defined using objective (e.g., cash flow coverage, debt-to-worth, etc.) and subjective (e.g., the quality of management, willingness to repay, etc.) factors.

- Ratings should reflect the risks posed by both the borrower's expected performance and the transaction's structure.

- The risk rating system should be dynamic — ratings should change when risk changes.

- The risk rating process should be independently validated (in addition to regulatory examinations).

- Banks should determine through back-testing whether the assumptions implicit in the rating definitions are valid   that is, whether they accurately anticipate outcomes. If assumptions are not valid, rating definitions should be modified.

- The rating assigned to a credit should be well supported and documented in the credit file.

Developments in Bank Risk Rating Systems

Many banks are developing more robust internal risk rating processes in order to increase the precision and effectiveness of credit risk measurement and management. This trend will continue as banks implement advanced portfolio risk management practices and improve their processes for measuring and allocating economic capital to credit risk. Further, expanded risk rating system requirements are anticipated for banks that assign regulatory capital for credit risk in accordance with the Basel Committee on Bank Supervision's proposed internal-ratings-based approach to capital. More and more banks are:

- Expanding the number of ratings they use, particularly for pass credits;

- Using two rating systems, one for risk of default and the other for expected loss;

- Linking risk rating systems to measurable outcomes for default and loss probabilities; and

- Using credit rating models and other expert systems to assign ratings and support internal analysis.

Pass Risk Ratings

Probably the most significant change has been the increase in the number of rating categories (grades), especially in the pass category. Precise measurement of default and loss probability facilitates more accurate pricing, allows better ALLL and capital allocation, and enhances early warning and portfolio management. Today's credit risk management practices require better differentiation of risk within the pass category. It is difficult to manage risk prospectively without some stratification of the pass ratings. The number of pass ratings a bank will find useful depends on the complexity of the portfolio and the objectives of the risk rating system. Less complex, community banks may find that a few pass ratings — for example, a rating for loans secured by liquid, readily marketable collateral; a "watch" category; and one or two other pass categories — are sufficient to differentiate the risk among their pass-rated credits. Larger, more complex institutions will generally require the use of several more pass grades to achieve their risk identification and portfolio management objectives.

Dual Rating Systems

In addition to increasing the number of rating definitions, some banks have initiated dual rating systems. Dual rating systems typically assign a rating to the general creditworthiness of the obligor and a rating to each facility outstanding. The facility rating considers the loss protection afforded by assigned collateral and other elements of the loan structure in addition to the obligor's creditworthiness. Dual rating systems have emerged because a single rating may not support all of the functions that require credit risk ratings. Obligor ratings often support deal structuring and administration, while facility ratings support ALLL and capital estimates (which affect loan pricing and portfolio management decisions).

The OCC does not advocate any particular rating system. Rather, it expects all rating systems to address both the ability and willingness of the obligor to repay and the support provided by structure and collateral. Such systems can assign a single rating or dual ratings. Whatever approach is used, a bank's risk rating system should accurately convey the risks the bank undertakes and should reinforce sound risk management.

Linking Internal and External (Public) Ratings

Public rating agencies provide independent credit ratings and analysis to keep the investment public informed about the credit condition of the obligors and instruments they rate. Banks' ability to purchase investment securities has long been tied to ratings supplied by "nationally recognized rating agencies"[2] under 12 USC 24. For the past several years, more and more loans are receiving public ratings, and banks are increasingly using public ratings in their risk management systems.

Banks are starting to map their internal risk ratings to public ratings. They use public ratings to create credit models and to fill gaps in their own default and loss data. Banks also obtain public ratings for loans and pools of loans to add liquidity to the portfolio. Public agency ratings are recognized and accepted in the corporate debt markets because of the depth of their issuer and default databases and because such ratings have been tested and validated over time. Appendix A defines the ratings used by the nationally recognized rating agencies.

While public agency ratings, bank ratings, and regulator ratings tend to respond similarly to financial changes and economic events, agency ratings may not have the same sensitivity to change that the OCC expects of bank risk ratings. Agency ratings can provide examiners one view of an obligor's credit risk; however, the examiner's risk rating must be based on his/her own analysis of the facts and circumstances affecting the credit's risk. Banks whose internal risk rating systems incorporate public agency ratings must ensure that their internal credit risk ratings change when risk changes, even if there has been no change in the public rating.

Automated Scoring Systems

While statistical models that estimate borrower risk have long been used in consumer lending and the capital markets, commercial credit risk models have only recently begun to gain acceptance. Increasing information about credit risk and rapid advances in computer technology have improved

---

[2] Currently, these agencies are Moody's Investor Services, Standard and Poor's Rating Agency, and Fitch.

modeling techniques for both consumer and commercial credit. Because of these advancements, the internal risk rating processes at some large banks can and do rely considerably on credit models. These banks use models to confirm internal ratings, assign finer ratings within broad categories, and supplement judgmentally assigned ratings. Most commercial credit scoring models attempt to estimate an obligor's probability of default and to assign a quantitative risk score based on those probabilities. Generally, they do not take into account a facility's structural elements, such as collateral, that can moderate the impact of a borrower's default.

Most credit scoring models are either statistical systems or expert systems:

1. A statistical system relies on quantitative factors that, according to the model vendor's research, are indicators of default. Examples of these models include Zeta®, KMV's Credit Monitor®, Moody's RiskCalc®, and Standard & Poor's CreditModel®.

2. An expert system attempts to duplicate a credit analyst's decision making. Examples include Moody's RiskScore® and FAMAS LA Encore® models.

One of the biggest impediments to the development of commercial credit scoring models has been the lack of data. Until recently, most banks did not maintain the data on commercial loan portfolios needed to develop the statistical analysis for modeling. However, after the credit events of the late 1980s and early 1990s, banks began to develop these databases. Because defaults and losses have been rare in recent years, constructing the databases with the number of observations necessary (thousands in some cases) has been difficult. Furthermore, these models have not yet been tested through a full business cycle. Whether they will be accurate during a recession, when safety and soundness concerns are most acute, remains a question.

Like other models, automated commercial credit scoring systems should be carefully evaluated and periodically validated. Until banks gain more experience with them under a range of market conditions, they should use such systems to supplement more traditional tools of credit risk management: credit analysis, risk selection at origination, and individual loan review. Additional information about models can be found in OCC Bulletin 2000 -

16, "Model Validation," dated May 30, 2000; the OCC's Risk Analysis Division (RAD) can also provide technical assistance.

Risk Rating Process Controls

A number of interdependent controls are required to ensure the proper functioning of a bank's risk rating process.

Board of Directors and Senior Management

The board and senior management must ensure that a suitable framework exists to identify, measure, monitor, and control credit risk. Board-approved policies and procedures should guide the risk rating process. These policies and procedures should establish the responsibilities of various departments and personnel. The board and management also must instill a credit culture that demands timely recognition of risk and has little tolerance for rating inaccuracy. Unless the board and senior management meet these responsibilities, their ability to oversee the loan portfolio can be severely hampered.

Staffing

The best and most important control over credit risk ratings is a well-trained and properly motivated staff. Personnel who rate credits should be proficient in the bank's rating system and in credit analysis techniques. These skills should be part of the bank's performance management system for credit professionals. Credit staff should be evaluated on, among other things, the accuracy and timeliness of their risk ratings.

Some banks assign the responsibility for rating credit exposures to their loan officers. Loan officers maintain close contact with the borrower and have access to the most timely information about their borrowers. However, their objectivity can be compromised by those same factors and their incentives are frequently geared more toward producing loans than rating them accurately.

Other banks address these problems by separating the credit and business development functions. This structure promotes objectivity, but a credit officer or analyst may not be as sensitive to subjective factors in a credit relationship as a loan officer. Many banks, therefore, find risk rating accuracy improves by requiring ratings to be a joint decision of lenders and credit officers (at least one person from each function). Whatever structure a bank adopts, the ultimate test of any rating process is whether it is accurate and effective. For this to occur, whoever assigns risk ratings needs good access to data and the incentive, authority, and resources to discharge this responsibility.

Reviewing and Updating Credit Risk Ratings

The benefits of rating risk are more fully realized if ratings are dynamic. The loan officer (or whoever is primarily responsible for rating) should review and update risk ratings whenever relevant new information is received. All credits should receive a formal review at least annually to ensure that risk ratings are accurate and up-to-date. Large credits, new credits, higher risk pass and problem credits, and complex credits should be reviewed more frequently.

In order to gain efficiencies, smaller, performing credits may be excluded from periodic reviews and reviewed as exceptions. Such loans tend to pose less risk transaction by transaction.

Management Information Systems

MIS are an important control because they provide feedback about the risk rating system. In addition to static data, risk rating system MIS should generate, or enable the user to calculate, the following information:

- The volume of credits whose ratings changed more than one grade (i.e., "double downgrades");

- Seasoning of ratings (the length of time credits stay in one grade);

- The velocity of rating changes (how quickly are they changing);

- Default and loss history by rating category;

- The ratio of rating upgrades to rating downgrades; and

- Rating changes by line of business, loan officer, and location.

MIS reports should display information by both dollar volume and item count, because some reports can be skewed by changes in one large account.

Credit Review

An independent third party should verify loan ratings. For many banks these verifications are conducted by credit review personnel, but other divisions or outsourcing may be acceptable. These verifications help to ensure accuracy and consistency, and augment oversight of the entire credit risk management process.

The verifications' formality and scope should correspond to the portfolio's complexity and inherent risk. The credit review function should be sufficiently staffed (both in numbers and in expertise) and appropriately empowered to independently validate and communicate the effectiveness of the risk rating system to the board and senior management. Smaller banks that do not have separate credit review departments can satisfy this requirement by using staff who are not directly involved with the approval or management of the rated credits to perform the review.

Internal Audit

Internal audit is another control point in the credit risk rating process. Typically, internal audit will test the integrity of risk rating data and review documentation. Additionally, they may test internal processes and controls for perfecting, valuing, and managing collateral; verify that other control functions, such as credit review, are operating as they should; and validate risk rating data inputs to the credit risk management information system.

Back-Testing

Systems that quantify risk ratings in terms of default probabilities or expected loss should be back-tested. Back-tests should show that the definitions' default probabilities and expected loss rates are largely confirmed by experience. Banks using credit models or other systems that use public rating agency default or transition information should demonstrate how their ratings are equivalent to agency ratings.

For those risk rating systems not explicitly tied to statistical probabilities, banks should be able to show that credits with more severe ratings exhibit higher defaults and losses. Although the default and loss levels are not explicitly defined in this type of rating system, the system should rank-order risk and should aggregate pools of similarly risky loans using an objective measurement of risk.

Examining the Risk Rating Process

Examiners evaluate a bank's internal risk rating process by considering whether:

- Individual risk ratings are accurate and timely.

- The overall system is effective relative to the risk profile and complexity of the bank's credit exposures.

To determine whether a bank's risk ratings are accurate, examiners will review a sample of loans and compare internal bank ratings with those assigned by OCC staff. Examiners should be most concerned when rating inaccuracies understate risk; however, any significant inaccuracy should be criticized because it will distort the picture of portfolio risk and diminish the effectiveness of interdependent portfolio management processes. Accurate risk ratings, in both the pass and problem categories, are critical to sound credit risk management, especially the determination of ALLL and capital adequacy.

When examiners discover significant risk rating inaccuracies (generally, greater than 5 percent of the number of credits reviewed, or 3 percent of the dollar amount), they must investigate to determine the root causes and decide whether to expand their loan review sample. Determining factors include:

- The nature and pattern of rating inaccuracies, for example, inaccuracies within pass categories, problem credits that are passed, missed ratings with a few large credits or several smaller credits, and inaccuracies in a specific portfolio or location;

- The severity of inaccuracy, i.e., how many grades away the rating is from what it should be;

- The adequacy of the ALLL and capital; and

- Whether inaccurate risk ratings distort overall portfolio risk and the bank's financial statements.

Examiners' analysis of risk rating accuracy and the bank's agreement or disagreement should be documented on an OCC line sheet and, if necessary, in a formal write-up for the Report of Examination. Credit write-up guidance and examples can be found in appendix B.

Reviewing the ratings of individual credits discloses much about how well the overall process is functioning. In their review of the risk rating process, examiners should determine:

- Whether there is a sufficient number of ratings to distinguish between the various types of credit risk the bank assumes;

- The effectiveness of risk rating process controls;

- Whether line lenders, management, and key administrative and control staff understand and effectively use and support the risk rating process; and

- The effectiveness of the risk rating system as a part of the bank's overall credit risk management process.

Whether reviewing individual credit ratings or the risk rating process, examiners should be alert for impediments or disincentives that may prevent the system from functioning properly. Such situations may include:

- Compensation programs that fail to reinforce lenders' and management's responsibility to properly administer, analyze, and report the risk in their portfolios. Worse yet, compensation programs that encourage lenders and management to understate risk in order to boost risk-adjusted returns or to generate incremental business by lowering risk-based pricing.

- Relationship management structures that may encourage lenders and management to "hide" problems for fear of losing control over a customer relationship (e.g., having to transfer management responsibilities to a workout division or specialist).

- Inexperience, incompetence, or unfounded optimism among lenders and management. Some account officers and managers have lent money only when the economy is favorable and may not be adept at recognizing or handling problems. Others may be unduly optimistic and may overlook obvious signs of increased risk.

Whatever the cause, it can be relatively easy for loan officers and line managers to rate credits a step, or more, above what they deserve. When examiners encounter such practices, they must ensure that required corrective actions address the root cause of the problem.

Rating Credit Risk

Examiners rate credit risk and expect national banks to rate credit risk based on the borrower's expected performance, i.e., the likelihood that the borrower will be able to service its obligations in accordance with the terms. Payment performance is a future event; therefore, examiners' credit analyses will focus primarily on the borrower's ability to meet its future debt service obligations. Generally, a borrower's expected performance is based on the borrower's financial strength as reflected by its historical and projected balance sheet and income statement proportions, its performance, and its future prospects in light of conditions that may occur during the term of the loan. Expected performance should be evaluated over the foreseeable future

— not less than one year. While the borrower's history of meeting debt service requirements must always be incorporated into any credit analysis, risk ratings will be less useful if overly focused on past performance. Credit risk ratings are meant to measure risk rather than record history. An example follows:

> A business borrower is in the third year of a seven-year amortizing term loan. The borrower has enjoyed good business conditions and financial health since the inception of the loan, has made payments as scheduled, and is current. However, the borrower's business prospects and financial capacity are weakening and are expected to continue to weaken in the upcoming year. As a result, the borrower's projected cash flow will be insufficient to cover the required debt service. In this simple example, the risk rating should be changed now when the borrower's risk of default increases rather than later when cash flow coverage becomes negative or when default occurs.

When credits are classified because of the borrower's or credit structure's well-defined weaknesses, examiners normally will await correction of the weaknesses and a period of sustained performance under reasonable repayment terms before upgrading the credit rating. The mere existence of a plan for improvement, by itself, does not warrant an upgrade.

For certain types of loans, however, examiners will base their risk ratings on a combination of the loans' current and historical performance. Such loans include retail credits (see page 19, "Uniform Retail Credit Classification and Account Management Policy") and smaller (as a percentage of capital) commercial loans amortizing in accordance with reasonable repayment terms. These loans, which normally will not be reviewed individually, will be classified based on their performance status and the quality of the underwriting.

The primary consideration in examiners' credit risk assessment is the strength of the primary repayment source. The OCC defines primary repayment source as a sustainable source of cash. This cash, which must be under the borrower's control, must be reserved, explicitly or implicitly, to cover the debt obligation. In assigning a rating, examiners assess the strength of the borrower's repayment capacity, in other words, the probability of default, where default is the failure to make a required payment in full and on time (see appendix C). As the primary repayment source weakens and default probability increases, collateral and other protective structural elements have a greater bearing on the rating.

The regulatory definition of substandard (see page 17) illustrates this progression. Examiners first assess the paying capacity of the borrower; then, they analyze the sound worth of any pledged collateral. Almost all credit transactions are expected to have secondary or even tertiary sources of repayment (collateral, guarantor support, third-party refinancing, etc.). Despite the secondary support, the rating assessment, until default has occurred or is highly probable, is generally based on the expected strength of the primary repayment source. In some instances, loans are so poorly structured that they require classification even though the likelihood of default is low. Examples are loans with deferred interest payments or no meaningful amortization.

Examiners will assign a rating to each credit that they review. The assigned rating applies to the amount that the bank is legally committed to fund. To determine this amount, an examiner may need to review the promissory note, loan agreement, or other such contract used to document the credit transaction. Ratings assigned to unfunded balances are designated "contingent."

Because the amount of credit risk is based on the borrower's expected performance over the foreseeable future, examiners will assess performance expectations over at least the upcoming 12 months. However, examiners will incorporate all relevant factors in a credit rating, regardless of timing conventions.

Assigning Regulatory Credit Classifications

The regulatory agencies use a common risk rating scale to identify problem credits. The regulatory definitions are used for all credit relationships — commercial, retail, and those that arise outside lending areas, such as from capital markets. The regulatory ratings special mention, substandard, doubtful, and loss identify different degrees of credit weakness. Credits that are not covered by these definitions are "pass" credits, for which no formal regulatory definition exists, i.e., regulatory ratings do not distinguish among pass credits. Examiners are expected to assign ratings in accordance with the guidance in this booklet, regardless of the system the bank employs.

Regulatory Definitions [3]

> Special mention (SM) — "A special mention asset has potential weaknesses that deserve management's close attention. If left uncorrected, these potential weaknesses may result in deterioration of the repayment prospects for the asset or in the institution's credit position at some future date. Special mention assets are not adversely classified and do not expose an institution to sufficient risk to warrant adverse classification."

Special mention assets have potential weaknesses that may, if not checked or corrected, weaken the asset or inadequately protect the institution's position at some future date. These assets pose elevated risk, but their weakness does not yet justify a substandard classification. Borrowers may be experiencing adverse operating trends (declining revenues or margins) or an ill-proportioned balance sheet (e.g., increasing inventory without an increase in sales, high leverage, tight liquidity). Adverse economic or market conditions, such as interest rate increases or the entry of a new competitor, may also support a special mention rating. Nonfinancial reasons for rating a credit exposure special mention include management problems, pending litigation, an ineffective loan agreement or other material structural weakness, and any other significant deviation from prudent lending practices.

The special mention rating is designed to identify a specific level of risk and concern about asset quality. Although an SM asset has a higher probability of default than a pass asset, its default is not imminent. Special mention is not a compromise between pass and substandard and should not be used to avoid exercising such judgment.

---

[3] Banking Circular 127 (Rev), issued in April 1991, contains the regulatory definitions for classified assets. Banking Bulletin 93-35, issued June 1993, contains the interagency supervisory definition of special mention assets.

Classified assets are exposures rated substandard, doubtful, or loss. Classified assets do not include pass and special mention exposures.

> Substandard C "A substandard asset is inadequately protected by the current sound worth and paying capacity of the obligor or of the collateral pledged, if any. Assets so classified must have a well-defined weakness, or weaknesses, that jeopardize the liquidation of the debt. They are characterized by the distinct possibility that the bank will sustain some loss if the deficiencies are not corrected."

Substandard assets have a high probability of payment default, or they have other well-defined weaknesses. They require more intensive supervision by bank management. Substandard assets are generally characterized by current or expected unprofitable operations, inadequate debt service coverage, inadequate liquidity, or marginal capitalization. Repayment may depend on collateral or other credit risk mitigants. For some substandard assets, the likelihood of full collection of interest and principal may be in doubt; such assets should be placed on nonaccrual. Although substandard assets in the aggregate will have a distinct potential for loss, an individual asset's loss potential does not have to be distinct for the asset to be rated substandard.

> Doubtful C "An asset classified doubtful has all the weaknesses inherent in one classified substandard with the added characteristic that the weaknesses make collection or liquidation in full, on the basis of currently existing facts, conditions, and values, highly questionable and improbable."

A doubtful asset has a high probability of total or substantial loss, but because of specific pending events that may strengthen the asset, its classification as loss is deferred. Doubtful borrowers are usually in default, lack adequate liquidity or capital, and lack the resources necessary to remain an operating entity. Pending events can include mergers, acquisitions, liquidations, capital injections, the perfection of liens on additional collateral, the valuation of collateral, and refinancing. Generally, pending events should be resolved within a relatively short period and the ratings will be adjusted based on the new information. Because of high probability of loss, nonaccrual accounting treatment is required for doubtful assets.

Loss C "Assets classified loss are considered uncollectible and of such little value that their continuance as bankable assets is not warranted. This classification does not mean that the asset has absolutely no recovery or salvage value, but rather that it is not practical or desirable to defer writing off this basically worthless asset even though partial recovery may be effected in the future."

With loss assets, the underlying borrowers are often in bankruptcy, have formally suspended debt repayments, or have otherwise ceased normal business operations. Once an asset is classified loss, there is little prospect of collecting either its principal or interest. When access to collateral, rather than the value of the collateral, is a problem, a less severe classification may be appropriate. However, banks should not maintain an asset on the balance sheet if realizing its value would require long-term litigation or other lengthy recovery efforts. Losses are to be recorded in the period an obligation becomes uncollectible.

Split Ratings

At times, more than one rating is needed to describe the risk in a credit exposure. One part of an exposure may require a more severe rating, hence the "split rating." Split ratings are usually assigned when collateral or other structural protection supports only part of the credit.

Three common split ratings are substandard/doubtful/loss, pass/adverse rating, and partial charge-off:

- Substandard/doubtful/loss C Assigned to collateral-dependent loans when the collateral's value is uncertain and falls within a range of values. The portion of the loan supported by the lower, more conservative value is rated substandard; the portion supported by higher, less certain value is classified doubtful; and any portion outside the range of values is loss.

- Pass/adverse rating C Assigned when a portion of a credit has an unquestionable repayment source and the remainder exhibits potential or well-defined credit weaknesses. This split rating is used for a loan partially secured with cash or other liquid collateral, such as listed securities, commodities, or livestock, provided the bank has reasonable controls in place that mitigate the risk of an out-of-trust sale. An unconditional "payment" guarantee (see appendix D) from a responsible, liquid, and creditworthy third party may also be included in this category.

- Partial charge-off C Assigned when the recorded balance of a partially charged-off loan is being serviced (payment sources are reliable and performance is sustained) and can reasonably be expected to be collected in full. The residual balance may deserve a pass rating or a special mention or other adverse rating may be appropriate if potential or well-defined weaknesses remain.

Rating Specialized Credits

Some specialized types of lending have unique attributes that examiners must consider when assigning a risk rating. When rating specialized commercial credits, examiners should follow the guidance in the following booklets of the Comptroller's Handbook:

- "Commercial Real Estate and Construction Lending," November 1995;
- "Leasing Finance," January 1998;
- "Agricultural Lending," December 1998; and
- "Accounts Receivable and Inventory Financing," March 2000.

Retail Credit. The same rating principles are used for retail and commercial loans, but the principles are applied differently for retail loans. Because retail credits are usually relatively small-balance, homogeneous exposures, the Federal Financial Institutions Council (FFIEC) agencies rate retail credits primarily on payment performance. Payment performance is a proxy for the strength of repayment capacity. This approach promotes consistency and efficiency.

Classification guidance for retail credit is detailed in the FFIEC's "Uniform Retail Credit Classification and Account Management Policy" (Uniform Policy) issued June 20, 2000. This policy statement establishes standards for classification of retail credit based on delinquency status, loan type, collateral protection, and other events influencing repayment, such as bankruptcy, death, and fraud. Examiners should refer to the Uniform Policy for details.

While the Uniform Policy should be followed in most circumstances, examiners always have the prerogative to rate a retail credit's risk more stringently, if appropriate, regardless of its payment status or collateral position. A harsher rating may be appropriate when underwriting standards or risk selection standards are compromised at loan inception, when the poor performance of a portfolio or individual transactions is masked by liberal cure programs (re-aging, extensions, deferrals, or renewals), or when a review of borrower repayment capacity justifies such a rating.

Foreign Assets. The evaluation of a bank's foreign assets must include a number of special considerations. Country risk factors, such as political, social, and macroeconomic conditions and events that are beyond the control of individual counterparties, can adversely affect otherwise good credit risks. For example, depreciation in a country's exchange rate increases the cost of servicing external debt and can increase the credit risk associated with even the strongest counterparties in a foreign country.

For countries in which the aggregate exposure of U.S. banks is considered significant, the Interagency Country Exposure Review Committee (ICERC) evaluates and assigns ratings for "transfer risk." The ICERC-assigned transfer risk ratings are applicable to most types of foreign assets held by an institution. In general, and except as noted in the more detailed discussion of this topic in appendix E, the ICERC-assigned transfer risk ratings are:

- The only ratings applicable to sovereign exposures in a reviewed country and

- The least severe risk rating that can be applied to all other cross-border and cross-currency exposures of U.S. banks in an ICERC-reviewed country.

However, because transfer risk is only one component of country risk, examiners should not criticize banks whose internally assigned risk rating for a country is more severe than the ICERC-assigned transfer risk rating. And because the ICERC does not evaluate the credit risk of individual private sector exposures in a country, examiners may assign such exposures credit risk ratings that are more severe than the country's ICERC-assigned transfer risk rating. For any given private sector exposure, the applicable rating is the more severe of either the ICERC-assigned transfer risk rating for the country or the examiner-assigned credit risk rating (including ratings assigned by the Shared National Credit Program).

Refer to appendix E and the "Guide to the Interagency Country Exposure Review Committee Process," issued in November 1999, for additional information on the special considerations and rules that are applicable in banks with foreign exposures.

Loans Purchased at a Discount. When a bank purchases a loan at a discount, the loan's book value will be less than the contract amount. Such a loan should receive a thorough credit risk evaluation and be assigned a rating that reflects its default probability and loss potential. Before a pass rating is assigned to a discounted loan, the reduced book value must sufficiently offset any weakened repayment capacity, high leverage, strained liquidity, or structural weakness.

Investment Securities. Information about the classification of investment securities is contained in BC 127 (rev), "Uniform Agreement on the Classification of Assets and Appraisal of Securities Held by Banks," April 26, 1991 and FAS 115, "Accounting for Certain Investments in Debt and Equity Securities."

The Credit Risk Evaluation Process

The risk rating process starts with a thorough analysis of the borrower's ability to repay and the support provided by the structure and any credit risk mitigants. When analyzing the risk in a credit exposure, examiners will consider:

- The borrower's current and expected financial condition, i.e., cash flow, liquidity, leverage, free assets;

- The borrower's ability to withstand adverse, or "stressed," conditions;

- The borrower's history of servicing debt, whether projected and historical repayment capacity are correlated, and the borrower's willingness to repay;

- Underwriting elements in the loan agreement, such as loan covenants, amortization, and reporting requirements;

- Collateral pledged (amount, quality, and liquidity), control over collateral, and other credit risk mitigants; and

- Qualitative factors such as the caliber of the borrower's management, the strength of its industry, and the condition of the economy.

Financial Statement Analysis

There is no substitute for rigorous analysis of a borrower's financial statements. The balance sheet, income statement, sources and uses of funds statement, and financial projections provide essential information about the borrower's initial and ongoing repayment capacity. Quantitative analysis of revenues, profit margins, income and cash flow, leverage, liquidity, and capitalization should be sufficiently detailed to identify trends and anomalies that may affect borrower performance.

The balance sheet deserves as much attention as the income statement. The balance sheet can provide an early warning of credit problems, for example, if assets degrade or the relative level of assets and liabilities changes. Commercial borrowers generate their revenue, income, and liquidity from their assets, so examiners should analyze the composition of these accounts and how their proportions change. Capitalization and liquidity also warrant careful analysis because they imply a borrower's ability to withstand an economic slowdown or unplanned events.

Cash Flow

Business cash flow is the operating revenue derived from ordinary business activities less operating costs paid (not simply incurred), plus noncash expenses such as depreciation and amortization. Although the concept is simple, cash flow calculations are often complex. Many businesses calculate cash flow differently because of the nature of their operations and cash conversion cycle.

Changes in "working capital" accounts should be reviewed to understand the cash flow implications. Uses of cash flow should be scrutinized — debt repayment is not the only use of cash flow. Changes, actual or planned, in capital expenditures must be closely reviewed. A troubled borrower will often cut capital expenditures in order to generate cash for debt service. Although this may provide short-term relief, such reductions can imperil a business's future. Shortfalls in cash flow or debt service coverage are usually the most obvious indications of a problem credit.

Ratio Analysis and Benchmarks

Financial ratios provide vital information about balance sheet and income statement proportions (debt to equity, income to revenues, etc.). Comparing a borrower's financial ratios with prior periods and industry or peer group norms can identify potential weaknesses. Whenever a ratio deviates significantly from that of its peers, examiners should conduct further analysis to identify the root cause.

Analysis of Projections

While current and historical information is necessary to establish a borrower's condition and financial track record, projections estimate expected performance. Examiners should analyze how projections vary from historical performance and assess whether the borrower is likely to achieve them. Projections should be analyzed under multiple scenarios — downside, break-even, best case, most likely case — and stress-tested periodically. Borrowers that quickly or repeatedly fall short of their projections lack credibility. Examiners' conclusion that a borrower will not be able to perform at projected levels should be factored into the loan's risk rating.

Other Repayment Sources

When economic and business conditions are favorable, lenders and borrowers often start to take for granted refinancing and recapitalization as a source of repayment. Such assumptions may be reasonable for consistently strong borrowers who have demonstrated access to credit and capital markets even during periods of economic distress. Weaker borrowers, however, need more reliable repayment sources because their access to these markets is often significantly diminished during economic downturns. In either case, loans for which refinancing is a source of repayment should only be made if the borrower has the capacity to repay the loan either through business cash flow or the liquidation of assets. In addition, a loan whose repayment continually relies on refinancing (often referred to as "evergreen loans") or whose borrower fails to achieve successful recapitalizations requires added scrutiny. Such loans are speculative at best and may warrant an adverse rating.

Other secondary repayment sources, such as collateral and guarantees, are discussed in the "Credit Risk Mitigants" section that follows.

Qualitative Considerations

Underwriting

Underwriting is the process by which banks structure a credit facility to minimize risks and generate optimal returns for the risks assumed. Sound underwriting provides protections such as coordinating repayment with cash flow, covenants, and collateral, thereby increasing the likelihood of collection. When competition or other pressures cause a bank to weaken its underwriting and structural protections, credit risk increases. Although structural weaknesses may not have an immediate effect on performance, they do affect the probability and severity of future problems.

At times, structural weaknesses can be so severe that the loan deserves an SM rating or classification. Examiners should not defer or forgo criticism of fundamental underwriting flaws because they have become the "competitive norm." For a detailed list of common structural weaknesses, see appendix F.

Management

The importance of a business borrower's management — competency and integrity— can not be overstated. The ability of the commercial entity's managers to guide it, exploit opportunities, develop and execute plans, and react to market changes is extremely important to its financial well being. The unexpected loss of one or two key employees can be detrimental to a company, particularly a small or mid-size firm. Even the most experienced management teams can be challenged by high growth, which is one of the most common reasons for business failure.

Industry

The purpose of industry analysis is to understand the conditions in which a business operates and the changes — cyclical, competitive, and technological— that it is likely to experience. Most industries exhibit some degree of cyclical volatility and some industries are exposed to seasonal variances, too. Such volatility affects the operating performance and financial condition of a company. Technological change and new competitors or substitute products can also affect performance.

Credit Risk Mitigation

Credit risk can be moderated by enhancing the loan structure. Parties to a loan can arrange for mitigants such as collateral, guarantees, letters of credit, credit derivatives, and insurance during or after the loan is underwritten. Although these mitigants have similar effects, there are important distinctions, including the amount of loss protection, that must be considered when assigning risk ratings. For example, a letter of credit may affect a loan's risk rating differently than a credit derivative.

Credit mitigants primarily affect loss when a loan defaults (see appendix C) and, except for certain guarantees, generally do not lessen the risk of default. Therefore, their impact on a rating should be negligible until the loan is classified. Examiners should be alert for ratings that overstate how much of a loan's credit risk is mitigated. Account officers at times assign less severe ratings based on the existence of collateral or other mitigants rather than undertaking a realistic assessment of the value the bank can recover.

The following discussion of the primary forms of mitigation provides guidance for determining an appropriate rating for a credit with a weak or potentially weak borrower and a credit mitigant. There are few hard and fast rules. Examiners should consider each credit facility separately, giving due consideration to every factor in the rating.

Collateral

Collateral, the most common form of credit risk mitigation, is any asset that is pledged, hypothecated, or assigned to the lender and that the lender has the right to take possession of if the borrower defaults. The lender's rights must be perfected through legal documents that provide a security interest, mortgage, deed of trust, or other form of lien against the asset. The process of perfecting the lender's interest varies by type of asset and by locality.

Once the lender has taken possession of the collateral, loan losses can be reduced or eliminated through sale of the assets. The level of loss protection is a function of the assets' value, liquidity, and marketability. Realistic collateral valuation is important at loan inception and throughout the loan's life, but it becomes increasingly important as the borrower's financial condition and performance deteriorate. Collateral valuations should include analysis of the value under duress — that is, what will the collateral be worth when it must be liquidated. The appropriate value may be a fair market, orderly liquidation, or forced liquidation valuation, depending on the borrower's circumstances. Rarely will a "going concern" valuation be appropriate when a loan becomes collateral-dependent. Proceeds from the sale will be diminished by costs related to repossession, holding, and selling the assets. Examiners should assess the validity of the bank's methods of valuing the collateral and determine whether the resulting values are reasonable.

When financial results show that the borrower is not able to repay the loan as structured, the loan should be considered collateral-dependent, classified, and reserved for in accordance with FAS 114, "Accounting by Creditors for Impairment of a Loan." Absent other credit risk mitigation, the portion of the loan covered by the proceeds from liquidating conservatively valued collateral normally should be classified substandard. Any remaining loan balance should be classified doubtful or loss depending on other factors.

Loan Guarantees

Loans may be guaranteed by related or unrelated businesses and individuals. Guarantor strength is often a major consideration when deciding whether to grant a loan, especially to start-up businesses. A guarantor's financial statement should be analyzed to ensure that the guarantor can perform as required, if necessary, and that the statement acknowledges the guarantee. Because the by-laws of some corporations prohibit them from assuming contingent liabilities, examiners may need to determine whether a guarantee is properly authorized.

Guarantee agreements should be as precise as possible, stating the specific credit facilities being guaranteed, under what circumstances the guarantor will be expected to perform, and what benefit the guarantor received for providing the guarantee. Guarantees can be unconditional or conditional. An unconditional guarantee generally extends liability equal to that of the primary obligor; in other words, the guarantor assumes the full responsibilities of the borrower. A conditional guarantee requires the creditor to meet a condition before the guarantor becomes liable. Guarantees can also be limited to a specific transaction, in amount, to interest or principal, and in duration. (Refer to appendix D for a brief description of common guarantees)

If a guarantee is to enhance a credit's risk rating, the guarantor must display the capacity and willingness to support the debt. A presumption of willingness is usually appropriate until financial support becomes necessary. At that point, willingness must be demonstrated. Once demonstrated, a strong guarantee can mitigate the risk of default or loss and justify a more favorable rating, despite an obligor's well-defined weaknesses. When adequate evidence of guarantor performance is lacking, the guarantee should not have a beneficial effect on the risk rating. Guarantors who attempt to invalidate their obligations through litigation or protracted renegotiations retard, rather than improve, a loan's collectibility.

Government guarantees are a special case. Credits with a U.S. government agency guarantee are usually accorded a pass rating. Most government guarantees are conditioned on bank management's performance (proper diligence and reporting), and mismanagement can void the guarantee and eliminate the rating enhancement. Although the incidence of mismanagement is very low, a rating enhancement may not be appropriate for banks with significant credit administration problems affecting the guaranteed credits. State or municipal guarantees usually have the same effect as U.S. government guarantees, although the bank must analyze and document the financial strength of these government entities. Guarantees from foreign governments require analysis of sovereign risk.

"Comfort letters," a common convention in international financing, are statements, usually from a domestic parent company, acknowledging a foreign subsidiary's debt. Many bankers maintain that comfort letters are guarantees, structured to avoid accounting conventions that require the parent to reflect guaranteed debt on its own financial statements. However, comfort letters are not legally binding, and in some instances they have not been honored. Therefore, they generally do not enhance a credit's rating. But when the parent has a demonstrated track record of honoring such commitments, or has a strong continuing interest in maintaining the financial condition of the borrowing entity, a comfort letter might enhance a risk rating. For example, if the borrower is the parent's sole supplier of an essential manufacturing component, risk is probably mitigated and the loan rating can be improved.

Letters of Credit

- A letter of credit (L/C) is a form of guarantee issued by a financial institution. An L/C rarely protects against default risk, unless it specifically can be drawn on for loan payments. An L/C issuer is typically more creditworthy than a guarantor. When an L/C that protects against default is obtained from a high-quality institution, it may effectively prevent default and losses. The issuer's low credit risk substantially mitigates the borrower's higher credit risk. Before a loss scenario could develop, both the borrower and the L/C issuer would have to default.

- The risk rating of a credit that is backed by an L/C issued by a high-quality institution generally should be rated no worse than substandard. However, examiners should evaluate the specific conditions that a borrower must meet before the L/C can be drawn on. When there is a distinct possibility that the borrower will fail to meet those conditions, the L/C should not have a beneficial effect on the rating.

An L/C can be irrevocable, which means all parties must agree to its cancellation, or revocable, which means the L/C can be canceled or amended at the discretion of the issuer. Revocable letters do not mitigate credit risk.

A standby L/C pays only when the obligor fails to perform. Examiners should evaluate the protections provided by a standby L/C just as they do that of other L/Cs.

Credit Derivatives

Credit derivatives can be used to manage capital, manage loan portfolios, and mitigate risk in individual transactions. Only credit derivatives for individual transactions have a bearing on risk ratings. Most of these credit derivatives mitigate loss, but they do not materially mitigate default risk.

Credit derivatives for individual loan transactions are usually purchased after the loan has been underwritten. In a typical credit derivative transaction, the protection purchaser (the creditor bank), for a fee, transfers some or all of a loan's credit risk to the protection seller. Standard types of derivatives are credit default swaps, total return swaps, credit-linked notes, and credit spread options.

Credit derivatives have unique structural characteristics and complexities that can diminish or eliminate their ability to reduce credit risk. In determining how much a derivative enhances a credit's rating (if indeed it does so at all), examiners should determine whether the derivative's protection is compromised by any of the following circumstances:

- The events that trigger payment are tied to a reference asset that may have different terms and conditions than the loan held by the bank. The residual exposure in this transaction is known as basis risk.

- The bank has forward credit exposure because the derivative has a shorter maturity than the bank loan. A timing mismatch can also occur when the protection does not take effect until some future date.

- The derivative has a materiality clause that limits protection to amounts over a designated threshold. In other words, the bank retains the first loss position.

- The definition of default or any other credit event that triggers the seller's payment is less rigorous for the swap or the reference asset than for the bank's loan. This is known as contract basis risk.

- The protection seller is materially at risk of default. If this seller and the reference asset are correlated (that is, if they are subject to many of the same economic and market forces), the risk to the protection buyer increases.

- Language in credit derivatives' contracts is complex and can be subject to different interpretations.

Credit Insurance

Credit insurance, a recent innovation for commercial loans, is not yet used extensively. Examiners should look for coverage-limiting insurance underwriting specifications such as deductible amounts and exclusion of certain loss events. Additionally, the insurer's financial strength and default risk should be evaluated. If the underwriting is acceptable and the insurer is strong, insurance can enhance a credit's risk rating in much the way an L/C does.

Accounting Issues

Accounting issues are intertwined with credit risk ratings, particularly at the classified level where the credit risk rating often dictates the accounting treatment. A brief discussion of accounting issues follows. For more detailed discussion of these topics refer to the OCC's "Bank Accounting Advisory Series" publications, Consolidated Reports of Condition and Income (call report) instructions, and Financial Accounting Standards Board (FASB) statements.

Rebooking Charged-off Credit

In 1997, the instructions to the call report were brought into compliance with generally accepted accounting principles (GAAP) and the practice of rebooking charged-off loans was disallowed. Under GAAP, when a bank charges off a loan or lease in part or full, the bank establishes a new cost basis. Once the loan's cost basis has been decreased, it cannot be increased later. For additional guidance concerning rebooking charged-off assets, refer to FASB 114, "Accounting by Creditors for Impairment of a Loan," and call report instructions.

Nonaccrual

A loan that is on nonaccrual or about to be placed on nonaccrual has severe problems such that the full collection of interest and principal is highly questionable. Nonaccrual loans will almost always be classified.

A bank places a loan on nonaccrual according to criteria in the call report instructions. The general rule is that an asset should be placed on nonaccrual when principal or interest is 90 days or more past due, unless the asset is well-secured and in the process of collection. A "well-secured" asset is secured by a lien or pledge of collateral that has a realizable value sufficient to discharge the debt fully (including accrued interest), or it is secured by the guarantee of a financially responsible party. An asset is "in the process of collection" if collection of the asset is proceeding in due course through legal action (including the enforcement of a judgment), or through efforts not involving legal action that are reasonably expected to result in the loan's repayment or in its restoration to a current status in the near future. A 30-day collection period has generally been applied to determining when a loan is "in the process of collection." Customarily, an asset can remain in that status more than 30 days only when it can be demonstrated that the timing and amount of repayment is reasonably certain.

There is no requirement that a loan must be delinquent for 90 days before it is placed on nonaccrual. Once reasonable doubt exists about a loan's collectibility, the loan should be placed on nonaccrual. When payment performance depends on the borrower drawing on lines of credit, the bank advancing additional loan funds, or the bank extending excessively lenient repayment terms, the loan should be considered for nonaccrual status. Loans propped up in this way are often referred to as "performing – nonperforming" loans. (For additional information, see "Capitalization of Interest" on page 33.) A borrower's financial statement can be adequate evidence of a high probability of default and exposure to loss; when it is, the loan should be placed on nonaccrual. While an asset is in nonaccrual status, some or all of the cash interest payments received may be treated as interest income on a cash basis as long as the remaining book balance of the asset is deemed to be fully collectible.

Consumer loans and loans secured by one- to four-family residential properties are not required to be placed on nonaccrual when the loan becomes 90 days delinquent. Each bank should formulate its own policies on these assets to ensure that net income is not being materially overstated. Examiners should evaluate the bank's accrual policy for these loans. In doing so, they should consider the portfolio size, 90-day roll rate to loss, and whether the nonaccrual criteria apply.

The call report instructions govern the reversal of previously accrued but uncollected interest and the treatment of subsequent payments on nonaccrual assets. When a loan is placed on nonaccrual, all previously accrued but uncollected interest should be reversed, unless the loan is secured by a U.S. government guarantee. For interest accrued in the current accounting period, the bank makes an adjusting entry directly against the interest income account. For prior accounting periods, the bank charges the ALLL if provisions for possible interest loss were made. If accrued interest provisions have not been made, the entire amount is charged against interest income.

An asset may be restored to accrual status when all principal and interest is current and the bank expects full repayment of the remaining contractual principal and interest, or when the asset otherwise becomes well-secured and is in the process of collection. The following assets do not have to meet these requirements to be restored to accrual status:

- Formally restructured loans qualifying for accrual status.

- Assets acquired at a discount from an unaffiliated third party.

- Loans that remain past due, but for which the borrower has resumed full payment of interest and principal according to contractual specifications.

Such loans qualify only if (1) all contractual amounts due can reasonably be expected to be repaid within a prudent period and (2) repayment has been in accordance with the contract for a sustained period (usually at least six months). For additional guidance see "Revised Interagency Guidance on Returning Certain Nonaccrual Loans to Accrual Status," appendix C in the "Commercial Real Estate and Construction Lending" booklet of the Comptroller's Handbook.

Capitalization of Interest

Interest may be capitalized (that is, accrued interest may be added to the principal balance of a credit exposure) for reporting purposes only when the borrower is creditworthy and has the ability to repay the debt in the normal course of business. Capitalization of interest is inappropriate for most classified loans. It should not be permitted if a loan is classified (by an examiner or the bank's internal risk rating process) (1) loss, (2) doubtful, (3) value-impaired,[4] or (4) nonaccrual. If interest has been inappropriately capitalized, the amount should be reversed or charged off in accordance with the methods permitted in the call report instructions. For additional guidance refer to Examining Circular 229, "Guidelines for Capitalization of Interest on Loans," dated May 1, 1985.

---

[4] A loan is impaired when, based on current information and events, it is probable that a creditor will be unable to collect all amounts due according to the contractual terms of the loan agreement.

Formally Restructured Loans

Restructured debt should be identified by the bank's internal credit review system and closely monitored by management. When analyzing a formally restructured loan, the examiner should focus on the borrower's ability to repay the credit in accordance with its modified terms.

The assignment of special mention status to a formally restructured credit would be appropriate if potential weaknesses remain after the restructuring. It would be appropriate to classify a formally restructured extension of credit adversely when well-defined weaknesses exist that jeopardize the orderly repayment of the credit under its modified terms. Restructured loans require a period of sustained performance, generally six months, under the restructured terms before being upgraded to a pass rating.

For a further discussion of troubled debt restructuring, see the glossary section of the call report instructions.

Loans Purchased at Discount

A bank purchasing a credit at a discount from its face amount must book the loan at the purchase price. Ordinarily, the discount is recognized as an adjustment of yield over the remaining contractual life of the loan. However, if the loan is acquired at a discount because full payment is not expected, the discount should be accounted for in accordance with the guidance in AICPA Bulletin 6, "Amortization of Discounts on Certain Acquired Loans," August 1989 (www.aicpa.org).

Appendix A: Nationally Recognized Rating Agencies Definitions

Moody's Investor Service
Long-Term Taxable Debt Ratings

"Aaa"   Debt rated "Aaa" is judged to be of the best quality. They carry the smallest degree of investment risk and are generally referred to as "gilt edged." Interest payments are protected by a large or by an exceptionally stable margin and principal is secure. While the various protective elements are likely to change, such changes as can be visualized are most unlikely to impair the fundamentally strong position of such issues.

"Aa"   Debt rated "Aa" is judged to be of high quality by all standards. Together with the "Aaa" group they comprise what is generally known as high-grade bonds. They are rated lower than the best bonds because margins of protection may not be as large as in Aaa securities or fluctuation of protective elements may be of greater amplitude or there may be other elements present which make the long-term risk appear somewhat larger than the "Aaa" securities.

"A"   Debt rated "A" possess many favorable investment attributes and are to be considered as upper-medium-grade obligations. Factors giving security to principal and interest are considered adequate, but elements may be present which suggest a susceptibility to impairment some time in the future.

"Baa"   Debt rated "Baa" is considered as medium-grade obligations (i.e., they are neither highly protected nor poorly secured). Interest payments and principal security appear adequate for the present but certain protective elements may be lacking or may be characteristically unreliable over any great length of time. Such bonds lack outstanding investment characteristics and in fact have speculative characteristics as well.

"Ba"   Debt rated "Ba" is judged to have speculative elements; their future cannot be considered as well assured. Often the protection of interest and principal payments may be very moderate, and thereby not well safeguarded during both good and bad times over the future. Uncertainty of position characterizes bonds in this class.

"B"   Debt rated "B" generally lack characteristics of the desirable investment. Assurance of interest and principal payments or of maintenance of other terms of the contract over any long period of time may be small.

"Caa"   Debt rated "Caa" is of poor standing. Such issues may be in default or there may be present elements of danger with respect to principal or interest.

"Ca"   Debt rated "Ca" represents obligations that are speculative in a high degree. Such issues are often in default or have other marked shortcomings.

"C"   Debt rated "C" is the lowest rated class of bonds, and issues so rated can be regarded as having extremely poor prospects of ever attaining any real investment standing.

Moody's ratings, where specified, are applicable to financial contracts, senior bank obligations and insurance company senior policyholder and claims obligations with an original maturity in excess of one year.

When the currency in which an obligation is denominated is not the same as the currency of the country in which the obligation is domiciled, Moody's ratings do not incorporate an opinion as to whether payment of the obligation will be affected by the actions of the government controlling the currency of denomination. In addition, risk associated with bilateral conflicts between an investor's home country and either the issuer's home country or the country where an issuer branch is located are not incorporated into Moody's ratings.

Moody's applies numerical modifiers "1," "2," and "3" in each generic rating classification from "Aa" through "Caa". The modifier "1" indicates that the obligation ranks in the higher end of its generic rating category; the modifier

"2" indicates a mid-range ranking; and the modifier "3" indicates a ranking in the lower end of that generic rating category.

Standard & Poor's
Long-Term Credit Ratings

"AAA"   An obligation rated "AAA" has the highest rating assigned by Standard and Poor's. The obligor's capacity to meet its financial commitment on the obligation is extremely strong.

"AA"   An obligation rated "AA" differs from the highest rated obligations only in small degree. The obligor's capacity to meet its financial commitment on the obligation is very strong.

"A"   An obligation rated "A" is somewhat more susceptible to adverse effects of changes in circumstances and economic conditions than obligations in higher rated categories. However, the obligor's capacity to meet its financial obligations is still strong.

"BBB"   An obligation rated "BBB" exhibits adequate protection parameters. However, adverse economic conditions, or changing circumstances are more likely to lead to a weakened capacity of the obligor to meet its financial commitment to the obligation.

Obligations rated "BB" through "C" are regarded as having significant speculative characteristics. "BB" indicates the least degree of speculation and "C" the highest. While such obligations will likely have some quality and protective characteristics, these may be outweighed by large uncertainties or major exposures to adverse conditions.

"BB"   An obligation rated "BB" is less vulnerable to nonpayment than other speculative issues. However, it faces major ongoing uncertainties or exposure to adverse business, financial, or economic conditions, which could lead to the obligor's inadequate capacity to meet financial commitment on the obligation.

"B" An obligation rated "B" is more vulnerable to nonpayment than obligations rated "BB," but the obligor currently has the capacity to meet its financial obligation. Adverse business, financial, or economic conditions will likely impair the obligor's capacity to or willingness to meet its financial commitment on the obligation.

"CCC" An obligation rated "CCC" is currently vulnerable to nonpayment, and is dependent upon favorable business, financial, and economic conditions for the obligor to meet its financial commitment on the obligation. In case of adverse business, financial, or economic conditions, the obligor is not likely to have the capacity to meet its financial commitment on the obligation.

"CC" An obligation rated "CC" is currently highly vulnerable to nonpayment.

"C" The "C" rating may be used to cover a situation where a bankruptcy petition has been filed or similar action has been taken, but payments on the obligation are being continued.

"D" The "D" rating, unlike other Standard & Poor's ratings, is not prospective; rather, it is used to only where a default has actually occurred – and not where a default is only expected.

The ratings from "AA" to "CCC" may be modified by the addition of a plus (+) or minus (-) sign to show relative standing within the major categories.

Fitch
Long-Term Credit Ratings

"AAA"   Highest credit quality. "AAA" ratings denote the lowest expectation of
           credit risk. They are assigned only in case of exceptionally strong
           capacity for timely payment of financial commitments. This capacity is
           highly unlikely to be adversely affected by foreseeable events.

"AA"   Very high credit quality. "AA" ratings denote a very low expectation of
           credit risk. They indicate very strong capacity for timely payment of
           financial commitments. This capacity is not significantly vulnerable to
           foreseeable events.

"A"   High credit quality. "A" ratings denote a low expectation of credit risk.
           The capacity for timely payment of financial commitments is
           considered strong. This capacity may, nevertheless, be more
           vulnerable to changes in circumstances or in economic conditions
           than is the case for higher ratings.

"BBB"   Good credit quality. "BBB" ratings indicate that there is currently a
           low expectation of credit risk. The capacity for timely payment of
           financial commitments is considered adequate, but adverse changes in
           circumstances and in economic conditions are more likely to impair
           this capacity. This is the lowest investment-grade category.

"BB"   Speculative. "BB" ratings indicate that there is a possibility of credit
           risk developing, particularly as the result of adverse economic change
           over time; however, business or financial alternatives may be available
           to allow financial commitments to be met. Securities rated in this
           category are not investment grade.

"B"   Highly speculative. "B" ratings indicate that significant credit risk is
           present, but a limited margin of safety remains. Financial commitments
           are currently being met; however, capacity for continued payment is
           contingent on a sustained, favorable business and economic climate.

"CCC,"   High default risk. Default is a real possibility. Capacity for meeting
"CC,"   financial commitments is solely reliant upon sustained, favorable

"C"   business or economic developments. A "CC" rating indicates that default of some kind appears probable. "C" ratings signal imminent default.

"DDD,"   Default. Securities are not meeting current obligations and are
"DD,"   extremely speculative. "DDD" designates the highest potential for
"D"   recovery of amounts outstanding on any securities involved. For U.S. corporates, for example, "DD" indicates expected recovery of 50 percent – 90 percent of such outstandings, and "D" the lowest recovery potential, i.e., below 50 percent.

Appendix B: Write-Up Standards, Guidelines, and Examples

Credit Write-up Comments

Credit write-ups inform the OCC and bank management about weaknesses within a bank, document the need for additional ALLL provisions, and support administrative actions. Write-ups support comments in the asset quality section of the examination report. For example, they often cite examples of liberal lending policies and practices, poorly structured credits, and problem loans that the bank has failed to identify. Write-ups also describe specific loans whose collectibility is questionable and which, if not collected, would have a significant effect on the bank's ALLL, earnings, or capital.

Loan write-ups assist bank management and board members by clearly communicating the reasons for credit classifications and credit administration deficiencies observed by examiners. Write-ups are valuable documentation when management's disagreement with criticisms or required corrective actions may result in remedial supervisory or enforcement actions (formal or informal) against the bank.

Write-ups are also an effective training tool and can help examiners determine the appropriate classification for a borderline credit. The informal rule is, "If in doubt, write it up." Writing up the pertinent credit factors will often guide the examiner toward the correct classification. If a write-up's conclusion is not well supported, further inquiry and analysis are often required to determine the appropriate classification.

If management and board members understand and are in general agreement with the examiner's classifications, conclusions, and recommended corrections, a write-up may not be necessary. EICs and LPMs should use their judgment to determine when write-ups are necessary.

Write-ups are generally recommended:

- For special mention and classified Shared National Credits,

---

- When the amount adversely rated, by borrower, exceeds the greater of $150,000 or 5 percent of capital,

- When management disagrees with the classification,

- When an insider loan is adversely rated, or

- When a violation of law is involved.

Loan write-ups are mandatory when a bank is, or may be, rated 3, 4, 5, and when any one of the last three items in the foregoing list applies. Additionally, for such banks, the threshold for adversely rated exposure is decreased to the greater of $100,000 or 2 percent of the bank's capital. These write-up criteria also should be considered for deteriorating 2-rated banks.

When a write-up is required, the examiner must present, in written form, comments pertinent to the loans and contingent liabilities subject to an adverse rating. Only matters relevant to the loan's adverse rating and collectibility should be discussed. An ineffective presentation of the facts weakens a write-up and frequently casts doubt on the accuracy of the risk assessment. The examiner should emphasize deviations from prudent banking practices, exceptions to policy, and administrative deficiencies that are germane to the credit's problems. When portions of a borrower's indebtedness are assigned different risk ratings, including those portions identified as pass, the comments should clearly set forth the reason for the split ratings. The essential test of a good write-up is whether it supports the rating.

Loan write-ups may be presented in a narrative or bullet format. Either format should summarize the credit, its weaknesses, and the reason for the rating. In order to prepare a succinct write-up, an examiner needs a thorough understanding of all pertinent matters.

Write-up Components

Write-ups generally consist of the five sections detailed below:

1. Heading

   - Outstanding balance, including contingent liabilities denoted by (c).
   - Accrued interest (usually only if charged-off).
   - Amount of previous charge-off(s).
   - Name of borrower.
   - Names of cosigners, guarantors, or endorsers.
   - Type of business.
   - Amount classified or rated special mention, entered under the appropriate column.
   - Previous OCC rating.
   - Bank's internal rating.

2. Credit Description

   - Type of facility.
   - Date originated.
   - Repayment terms.
   - Maturity date.
   - Restructure dates and terms (if applicable).
   - Purpose.
   - Collateral, including most recent valuation, valuation date, and source.
   - Source of repayment.
   - Delinquency and accrual status (dates or duration).

3. Financial Information

This section should include a synopsis of the credit weaknesses, the borrower's financial condition, and support for the classification. The examiner should present conclusions derived from analysis of the financial information rather than recite details. Using too many details from the financial statement and listing historical comparisons detracts from the write-up. Indicate the type of financial statement (personal/audited/unaudited) and date. Include a brief description of any support provided by cosigners, guarantors, or endorsers. If their support has not yet been drawn on, succinctly explain why.

4. Analysis

Be specific and factual, avoid speculation. Explain:

- The cause of the credit problem and the effect on the borrower's ability to repay.
- Current repayment source or the lack of a viable repayment source.
- Any economic conditions, industry problems, and other external factors that bear on the rating.
- Actions management has taken or will take to strengthen the credit.
- Actions management failed to take to supervise the credit properly.

5. Conclusion

- Reasons for the rating, including a clear distinction between split ratings.
- An explanation of differences between the outstanding balance and the rated amount (e.g., any portion secured by cash or other liquid collateral.)
- Any special instructions to management (e.g., additional ALLL provision, triggers to place the asset on nonaccrual, etc.)
- Whether management (identify the officer) agrees with the classification.
- If management (identify the officer) disagrees, explain why and your reasons for discounting their reasoning.

Abbreviated Comments

When write-ups are prepared, comments may be abbreviated at the discretion of the EIC, if:

- The bank's internal credit review program (or any other bank-sponsored review of assets) accurately identifies the credit weaknesses, or

- Examiners prepared a detailed write-up of the credit during a previous analysis.

In such cases, the abbreviated comments should include the borrower's name, business or occupation, type and amount of the loan, risk rating (including any significant change from the previous write-up), and a brief description of the reason for the assigned risk rating. The explanation for the risk rating usually should not exceed one or two sentences.

Write-up Examples

CREDITS SUBJECT TO CLASSIFICATION OR SPECIAL MENTION

Amount	SM	Substandard	Doubtful	Loss
7,900,000 TL		7,900,000		

BORROWER: TOWN OFFICE CENTER, LLP
Any Town, USA

LINE OF BUSINESS: Limited liability real estate partnership.

GUARANTORS/PARTNERS: No guarantors. General partner provides no outside financial support.

PREVIOUS DISPOSITION/NON-ACCRUAL DATE: Substandard 100%

TERMS:

ORIG/RENEWAL/MATURITY DATES:	Originated May-89 at 12MM; renewed Feb-92 at 11MM, renewed Dec-95 at 9MM, and renewed Dec-98 at 8MM; matures Dec-01.
IS INTEREST CURRENT? (Y/N):	Yes
PURPOSE OF LOAN:	Construct 6500 sf office building
CURRENT PAYMENT SCHEDULE:	Interest monthly plus 60% of excess cash flow payable quarterly.
INTEREST RATE/PRICING:	Prime + 100 bp
COLLATERAL:	1st REM on 4 story office building. Collateral controls allow for inspections and re-appraisals when needed; quarterly rent rolls and operating information.
COLLATERAL VALUATION/DATE:	Independent AV 9.5MM as of Jan-99
SOURCE OF REPAYMENT:	Project cash flow; secondarily, from refinance or sale of the property.
COMPLIANCE W/COVENANTS(Y/N)	No. Covenants restructured.

REASON(S) FOR DISPOSITION:

Bank originally financed construction of subject property through a line of credit. Permanent refinancing could not be obtained and credit was restructured into the current term structure. Below budget revenues resulted in noncompliance with leverage and minimum cash flow coverage covenants. Debt was restructured in accordance with borrower's diminished cash flow. FYE-98 NOI of 900M provided 1.3X interest coverage, but only nominal principal amortization. Further reduction in debt service capacity is possible given tenant rollover, the variable rate structure and lack of interest rate protection, and potential operating expenses increases.

Over the last three years, lease rollovers averaged 25% annually and market rents were flat, reducing the opportunity for increased NOI and increased principal payments. The projected loss of a major tenant within 18 months will further reduce the property's NOI. Significant marketing efforts are anticipated in order to re-lease the vacated space.

The project has an 83% LTV. Principals in the project have been unsuccessful in attracting external financing without additional equity and/or increased rents. Near term takeout prospects are remote and continued bank financing is likely.

Considered substandard due to insufficient cash flow to support permanent financing at market rates and terms, covenant defaults, and potential further cash flow deterioration if re-leasing of projected vacancy fails. Cash flow projections for the next 18 months reflect continued support under liberal restructured terms. VP Doe agreed with the classification.

November, 2000

As of May 17, 2012, this guidance applies to federal savings associations in addition to national banks.*

CREDITS SUBJECT TO CLASSIFICATION OR SPECIAL MENTION

Amount	SM	Substandard	Doubtful	Loss
1,095.090 RC (1)	1,095,090			
697,387 TL (2)	697,387			
1,892,477				

BORROWER: SOME BUSINESS INC. (SBI) (1)
JOHN DOE (2)

LINE OF BUSINESS: Retail Office Furniture

GUARANTORS/PARTNERS: John Doe

PREVIOUS DISPOSITION/NON-ACCRUAL DATE: Pass

John Doe owns SBI and the commercial real estate properties leased to SBI.

1) Outstanding balance of $1,100M working capital line of credit. Originated 5/99 and due on demand, with interest payable semi-annually; loan agreement contains no borrowing base controls. Secured by first lien on AR, INV and fixed assets. Collateral values are AR $813M (12/99 AR aging - current and less than 60 days past due), Inventory $321M 11/99 FS, and fixed assets $400M 11/99 FS, resulting in total value of this collateral package $1,534M. Collateral reflects balances after applying bank-lending margins of 75%, 60%, and 50% respectively.

2) Originated 1/99 at $700M, proceeds used to purchase commercial building and fund improvements. Monthly payments of $6,869 on a 15-year amortization are current. Collateral consists of a 1st REM on a commercial building located at 1 Main St., Anytown, USA, AV (9/99) $750M.

Interim losses through 11/99 have resulted in tight working capital and high leverage with debt to worth at 5.5X. Through eleven-months SBI posted a pretax loss of $110M and negative EBITDA of $19M. Interim loss was caused by SBI funding losses at a related business and a delay in the start of a significant contract. Contract work has now commenced and the related business has been closed. SBI's prior periods' earnings and cash flow had been strong with net profits of $238M and $259M in FY97 and FY98 respectively. Loan officer expects restoration of profitable operations in FY2000.

John Doe's personal FS dated 1/99 reflects NW $2.6MM centered in the business and real estate associated with this debt. Personal tax return for 1998 shows AGI $211M consisting primarily of wages $126M ($105M from SBI) and $85M rental income from subject commercial real estate. Rent paid to John Doe is adequate to service (2).

Special Mention - Historical strong performance and resolution of recent problems mitigate the interim operating losses and resultant high leverage and tight working capital. This rating also acknowledges the weak borrowing base controls. VP Smith agrees with the rating.

March, 2000

CREDITS SUBJECT TO CLASSIFICATION OR SPECIAL MENTION

Amount	SM	Substandard	Doubtful	Loss
262,094		230,300		32,094
23,750 Accrued Interest				23,750

BORROWER: DONALD FARMER

LINE OF BUSINESS: Crop farmer

GUARANTORS/PARTNERS: None

PREVIOUS DISPOSITION/NON-ACCRUAL DATE: Substandard 100%

Note represents the consolidation of term loans to finance 80 acres, farm machinery, and carryover debt. Note originated 1/98 at $270M and called for annual payments of $30M (principal and interest). The payment due on 1/00 was extended twice and is now due on 1/01. A recent farm inspection shows that collateral now consists of grain ($16M), M&E ($144M), and RE ($70M).

Borrower incurred addition debt in mid-1990's in order to expand his farming operation. After the expansion, the borrower's operation was negatively affected by three years of severe drought and low commodity prices. Unaudited 12/99 FS reports an illiquid and nearly insolvent position. Tax returns indicate profits and cash are insufficient to amortize the bank debt over a reasonable timeframe. Interim results show no improvement.

Classification reflects the following well-defined weaknesses: the borrower's inability to service the debt; an illiquid, under-capitalized financial position; and insufficient collateral. The portion of debt supported by collateral is classified substandard, the remaining balance is classified loss.   The $23,750 of accrued interest should also be charged off; the loan should be placed on nonaccrual as full collection of interest and principal is unlikely. Loan officer Doe concurs with the classification.

November, 2000

Appendix C: Rating Terminology

Many companies in the financial services industry use the following three terms when defining credit risk: probability of default (PD), loss given default (LGD), and expected loss (EL). While these terms are not used in the regulatory rating definitions, the concepts are inherent to the regulatory ratings. Probability of default measures repayment capacity — the higher the PD, the weaker the primary source of repayment. When repayment capacity exhibits well-defined weaknesses, analysis shifts to the strength of secondary sources and the potential, or expected, loss.

- Probability of Default - PD is the risk that the borrower will be unable or unwilling to repay its debt in full or on time. The risk of default is derived by analyzing the obligor's capacity to repay the debt in accordance with contractual terms. PD is generally associated with financial characteristics such as inadequate cash flow to service debt, declining revenues or operating margins, high leverage, declining or marginal liquidity, and the inability to successfully implement a business plan. In addition to these quantifiable factors, the borrower's willingness to repay also must be evaluated.

- Loss Given Default - LGD is the financial loss a bank incurs when the borrower cannot or will not repay its debt. The amount of loss is generally affected by the quality of the underwriting and the quality of management's supervision and administration. Underwriting standards define the structure of a loan (maturity, repayment schedule, financial reporting requirements, etc.) and establish conditions and protections that allow the bank to control the risk in the credit relationship. Such conditions and protections can include collateral and collateral margin requirements, covenants, and support required from guarantees and insurance.

  Generally, loss is defined using accounting-based conventions. Loss is the expectation that principal and interest will not be fully repaid after factoring in expected recovery amounts. Accounting "loss" is not the same as true economic loss, which also factors in the increased expenses associated with problem credits.

- Expected Loss - EL is the mathematical product of PD and LGD. Since both PD and LGD can vary in response to economic conditions, EL falls within a range of values over time.

Appendix D: Guarantees

A guarantee (also spelled guaranty) is the assurance that a contract will be duly carried out. For loans, a guarantee usually takes the form of a promise by a person or entity to pay the obligation of another party. While an unconditional (or absolute) guarantee affords a lender the greatest protection, conditional and limited guarantees also provide lenders valuable protections. Guarantees have a number of common forms:

- Contingent guarantees require a specific event to occur before the guarantor is liable.

- Continuing guarantees extend liability for an obligor's present and future debts. (Also called an open guarantee.)

- Collection guarantees extend liability only after default and is conditioned on the creditor first exhausting legal remedies against the obligor.

- Payment guarantees extend liability based on the debt's contractual terms. The lender does not have to first seek the primary obligor's performance. This type of guarantee mitigates risk of default.

- Irrevocable guarantees cannot be terminated without the consent of the other parties.

- Revocable guarantees can be terminated by the guarantor without any other party's consent.

- Declining guarantees reduce the guarantor's liability as certain conditions are met. For example, construction project guarantees are often linked to the construction's progress.

Appendix E: Classification of Foreign Assets

Banks doing business internationally must concern themselves not only with the risks associated with domestic operations but also with country risk and transfer risk. This appendix discusses the effect of these additional risks on the evaluation of foreign assets and provides guidance on the examination treatment of a bank's exposures to residents of foreign countries.

Country Risk

Country risk, which is associated with the obligations of both public and private sector counterparties in a foreign country, is the possibility that economic, social, and political conditions and events might adversely affect the bank's interests in a country. Country risk includes the possibility of deteriorating economic conditions, political and social upheaval, nationalization and expropriation of assets, government repudiation of external indebtedness, exchange controls, and currency depreciation or devaluation.

Country risk is an important consideration when determining how much credit risk is associated with individual counterparties in a country. Regardless of the availability of foreign exchange, political, social, and macroeconomic conditions and events that are beyond the control of individual counterparties can adversely affect otherwise good credit risks. Depreciation in a country's exchange rate, for example, increases the cost of servicing external debt; it can increase not only the level of transfer risk for the country, but also the credit risk associated with even the strongest counterparties in a country.

Country risk significantly affects the credit risk of many kinds of exposures, including:

- Direct exposures to foreign-domiciled counterparties;

- Direct exposures to U.S -domiciled counterparties whose creditworthiness is significantly affected by events in a foreign country;

- Direct exposures to U.S -domiciled counterparties when one of the determinants of value is a foreign country's foreign exchange or interest rate environment (e.g., when one rate in an interest rate swap is derived from a foreign country's yield curve); and

- Indirect exposures when the value of the underlying collateral or the creditworthiness of the guarantor is influenced by events in a foreign country.

Transfer Risk

Transfer risk is a subset of country risk that is evaluated by the Interagency Country Exposure Review Committee (ICERC). Transfer risk is the possibility that an asset cannot be serviced in the currency of payment because the obligor's country lacks the necessary foreign exchange or has put restraints on its availability.

Based on its evaluation of conditions in a country, the ICERC assigns transfer risk ratings of "strong," "moderately strong," "weak," "other transfer risk problems," "substandard," "value impaired," or "loss." [5]

The volume and transfer risk ratings of foreign exposures are relevant to any assessment of possible concentrations of risk and the adequacy of the bank's capital and allowance for loan and lease losses. In addition, exposures rated "value impaired" are generally subject to an allocated transfer risk reserve (ATRR) requirement.

Applicability of Transfer Risk Ratings

ICERC-assigned transfer risk ratings are applicable in every U.S-chartered, insured commercial bank in the 50 states of the United States, the District of Columbia, Puerto Rico, and U.S. territories and possessions. The ratings are also applicable in every U.S. bank holding company, including its Edge and Agreement corporations and other domestic and foreign nonbank

---

[5]See the "Guide to the Interagency Country Exposure Review Committee Process," which was issued in November 1999, for a comprehensive discussion of the operations of the ICERC. The guide is available on the OCC's public Web site at www.occ.treas.gov/icerc.pdf .

subsidiaries. Finally, the ratings are applicable in the U.S. branches and agencies of foreign banks (however, the ATRR requirement does not apply to these entities).

For purposes of the ICERC-assigned rating, the determination of where the transfer risk for a particular exposure lies takes into consideration the existence of any guarantees, and is based on the country of residence of the ultimate obligor as determined in accordance with the instructions for the FFIEC 009 "Country Exposure Report."

ICERC-assigned transfer risk ratings are:

- Applicable to all types of foreign assets held by an institution.

- The only rating that examiners may apply to a reviewed country's sovereign exposures (that is, direct or guaranteed obligations of the country's central government or government-owned entities).

- The least severe risk rating that can be applied to all other cross-border and cross-currency exposures of U.S. banks in a reviewed country.

The foregoing rules on applying ICERC-assigned transfer risk ratings are subject to the following exceptions:

- Bank premises, other real estate owned, and goodwill are not subject to the ICERC-assigned transfer risk ratings.

- Regardless of the currencies involved, to the extent that an institution's in-country offices have claims on local country residents that are funded by liabilities to local country residents, the ICERC-assigned transfer risk ratings do not apply. For example, to the extent that the London branch of a U.S. bank has liabilities to local residents (such as sterling deposits), the branch's claims on a public or private sector obligor in the United Kingdom (whether they be denominated in sterling, dollars, or marks) are not subject to the ICERC-assigned transfer risk rating.

- If they are carried on the institution's books as investments, securities issued by a sovereign entity in a country that is reviewed and rated by the ICERC are also subject to the FFIEC's "Uniform Agreement on the Classification of Assets and Appraisal of Securities Held by Banks." The FFIEC agreement provides for specific, and possibly more severe, classification of "sub-investment-quality securities."

- Except for sovereign securities that are carried on the institution's books as an investment (and, therefore, are subject to the guidance in the previous paragraph), sovereign exposures in countries that are not reviewed and rated by the ICERC are not subject to in-bank classification by the examiner (for either transfer or credit risk reasons). If the exposure in question is considered to be significant in relation to the bank's capital (generally greater than 10 percent), the examiner should consult with his or her supervising office on how to proceed.

Formal Guarantees and Insurance on Foreign Exposures[6]

It is not unusual for claims on obligors in a foreign country to be guaranteed or insured by a counterparty located in a different country. As noted earlier, such claims are subject to the transfer risk rating applicable to the country of the guarantor when the guarantor has formally obligated itself to repay if the direct obligor fails to do so for any reason B including transfer risk. Insurance policies are treated as guarantees provided they cover specific assets and guarantee payment if the borrower defaults or if payment can't be made in the stipulated currency for any reason, including both credit risk and country risk.

Questions have also been raised about how much regard should be given to the willingness and ability of guarantors to perform when evaluating cross-border exposure to a given country. The existence of a firm guarantee as described in part 1C of the instructions for the FFIEC 009 report (and also the instructions for the FFIEC 019 "Country Exposure Report for U.S. Branches and Agencies of Foreign Banks") provides the basis for the reporting

---

[6] See the instructions for preparation of the FFIEC 009 "Country Exposure Report" for a more detailed discussion of the treatment of guaranteed claims. The instructions are available on the FFIEC's public web site at www.ffiec.gov/ffiec_report_forms.htm#FFIEC009.

institution to reallocate an exposure from country A (the residence of the primary obligor) to country B (the residence of the guarantor) on its FFIEC 009 or FFIEC 019 country exposure report.

However, each reporting institution has a responsibility to adequately document the capacity and willingness of guarantors to honor their commitments. If an examiner subsequently determines that a guarantee does not mitigate credit risk and that reallocating the exposure to Country B on the country exposure report understates cross-border risk in Country A , then the institution should be directed to cease reallocating the exposure to Country B on future country exposure reports. Furthermore, the examiner may, for examination purposes, apply the transfer risk rating ICERC has assigned to Country A.

Distribution of ICERC Country Write-ups

Because the ICERC deliberations are part of the examination process, the committee's transfer risk ratings can be communicated only to those institutions that have exposures to the reviewed country.[7] Following each ICERC meeting, the committee routinely distributes write-ups for countries where exposures have been rated "other transfer risk problems" or worse. These write-ups go to banks, bank holding companies, and Edge and Agreement corporations that have reported exposure to the country on the most recent FFIEC 009 country exposure report. Write-ups for countries where exposures have been rated "moderately strong" or "weak" are not routinely distributed; however, they may be provided by the bank's examiner-in-charge or supervising office if there are concerns about the level of exposure to the country.

Because they are not required to file an FFIEC 009 country exposure report, some smaller U.S. banks and the U.S. branches and agencies of foreign banks do not routinely receive ICERC's country write-ups. Some institutions may have exposures that were not reported on the FFIEC 009 country exposure report, either because they were booked after the quarterly reporting date or

---

[7] The ICERC-assigned transfer risk ratings are primarily a supervisory tool. They are not intended to be used for credit allocation, nor should they replace a bank's own country risk analysis. For this reason, country write-ups are not provided to a bank unless it has exposure to the country.

were less than the reporting threshold (all amounts on the report are rounded to the nearest million dollars). In these cases, the bank may make a request to its examiner-in-charge or supervising office for the country write-ups applicable to its exposures.

Credit Risk on Foreign Exposures

As noted in the discussion of transfer risk, the ICERC-assigned transfer risk rating is the only rating examiners may apply to sovereign exposures in a reviewed country, unless the exposures are securities in an investment account. However, the ICERC is not able to evaluate the credit risk associated with individual private-sector exposures in a country. Therefore, based on an evaluation of credit risk factors (including the effects of country risk), examiners may assign credit risk ratings to individual private-sector exposures that are more severe than the ICERC-assigned transfer risk rating for the country. For any given private sector exposure, the applicable rating is the more severe of either the ICERC-assigned transfer risk rating for the country or the examiner-assigned credit risk rating (including ratings assigned by the Shared National Credit Program).

Examiners should be aware of two additional issues that arise primarily in the context of a bank's international activities. Those issues, which concern trade-related credits and informal or implied guarantees by central governments, are discussed below.

Trade-related Credits

Trade credit has traditionally been viewed as posing relatively low risk for banks. According to this view, the credit risk is low because the asset is self-liquidating and the transfer risk is low because economically distressed countries have historically given high priority to paying foreign trade obligations when allocating scarce international reserves to pay external debts.

However, trade credit has been less certain to self-liquidate in recent years. Difficult economic conditions in some countries have hindered importers seeking to sell their goods and to satisfy their obligations under letters of credit issued on their behalf. In other cases, economic conditions have so eroded the liquidity and solvency of some foreign banks that the institutions have delayed paying the U.S. banks that have confirmed their letters of credit, even when local importers have paid the original obligation. In some cases, U.S. banks have been forced to write off trade credits when they found themselves to be the unsecured creditor of a failed foreign bank and the country's banking authority was either unwilling or unable to promptly settle the bank's outstanding obligations.

As for transfer risk, the priority status of trade-related credits is not as meaningful as it once was. While a number of governments levied administrative controls to allocate foreign exchange reserves during the 1980s, most did not do so during the economic crises of the 1990s. Instead, reserves were generally available, but at very steep exchange rates. As a result, what was a transfer risk problem in the debt crises of the early 1980s is now apt to be a credit risk problem affecting even the strongest borrowers in a country.

The use of documentary trade credits appears to be declining. U.S. banks both large and small have increasingly relied on unsecured working capital credits to finance the trade-related activities of foreign correspondent banks and their customers. This may reflect a recognition of the fact that, in practice, the U.S. bank's credit risk on these types of transactions is more directly affected by the financial strength and credit worthiness of its foreign bank counterparty than by the underlying trade transaction.

Informal or Implied Guarantees

Examiners sometimes ask how much weight should be given to informal expressions of support by a country's central government for a particular borrower or category of credit (most often, trade-related credits). Unless these expressions of support constitute a guarantee or other legally binding commitment, examiners should view them as no more than a mitigating factor in their evaluation of the counterparty's credit risk. Informal expressions of support by the central government would not cause the ICERC-assigned transfer risk rating for the country to be substituted for the counterparty's credit risk rating.

When evaluating a central government's informal expressions of support and implied guarantees, consider:

- What standard is the government likely to apply in determining which credits it will support?

- How important is the obligor to the country's economy? (If the government does not have the capacity to support the entire stock of, for example, trade credit, how likely is it that the credit being evaluated will be selected for support?)

- How important is this U.S. bank's presence in the country, and is its role in the economy likely to influence the government's decision whether to support its obligors?

- If support is provided, how prompt is repayment likely to be?

Appendix F: Structural Weakness Elements

Excerpted from MM 98-30, "Examiner Guidance   Credit Underwriting," dated September 17, 1998

Structural weaknesses are underwriting deficiencies that can compromise a bank's ability to control a credit relationship if economic or other events adversely affect the borrower. Some degree of structural weakness may be found in virtually any aspect of a loan arrangement or type of loan, and the presence of one (or more) need not be indicative of an overall credit weakness deserving criticism. Instead, the examiner must evaluate the relative importance of such factors in the context of the borrower's overall financial strength, the condition of the borrower's industry or market, and the borrower's total relationship with the bank.

Some of the most prevalent structural weakness are:

- Indefinite or speculative purpose — The loan purpose should clearly reflect the actual use of the proceeds. Loans for ambiguous or speculative purposes deserve extra scrutiny. Loans in amounts over $5,000 not secured by an interest in real estate are required to have a purpose statement by 12 CFR103.33.

- Indefinite or overly liberal repayment program — Loans that lack a clear and reasonable repayment program (source and timing) present extra risk, regardless of their nominal maturity. This includes loans that revolve continually   "evergreen loans"   where the bank is essentially providing debt capital. Typical indicators of unrealistic repayment terms include: bullet maturities unrelated to the actual source of repayment funds, re-writes or renewals for the purpose of simply deferring a maturity, loans used to finance asset purchases with a repayment plan significantly in excess of the useful life of the asset, and advances to fund interest payments.

- Nonexistent, weak, or waived covenants — In large and mid-size banks, covenants are generally required for medium and longer term credits and can be an effective control mechanism. Effective covenants typically provide the lending bank with an opportunity to trigger protective action if a defined aspect of the borrower's operation or financial condition falls below prescribed standards. Examiners should be alert for covenants that have been waived or renegotiated by the bank to accommodate a borrower's failure to maintain the original standards. Community banks often make term loans without formal loan agreements or covenants; however, community bank management should be encouraged to make use of meaningful covenants for loans exceeding a certain dollar level.

- Inadequate debt service coverage — The initial underwriting of loans that are intended to be repaid from operating cash flow should provide for an acceptable margin to repay both principal and interest in a reasonable time based on historical performance. If repayment is predicated on new revenues that are expected to be enabled by the loan, then anticipated future cash flows should be reasonable and well documented.

- Elevated leverage ratio — Acceptable leverage ratios vary based on industry, loan purpose, covenant definition, CAPEX restrictions, and dividend payouts. Examiners should consider both the reasonableness of the leverage ratio and how it is defined. Leverage ratios may be calculated as debt to worth or debt to cash flow; industry standards prescribe which methodology is most appropriate.

- Inadequate tangible net worth — Companies need tangible net worth to sustain them during unforeseen, adverse situations. Consider both the absolute amount of tangible net worth and its amount relative to debt.

- Inadequate financial analysis — The level of analysis should be commensurate with the level of risk. If the loan approval documentation lacks sufficient analysis of financial trends, primary and secondary repayment sources, industry trends, and risk mitigants, the loan may fit this category. More complex credits normally should also require sensitivity analysis (base case, break event case, etc.) and risk/reward analysis.

- Insufficient collateral support — This occurs when the borrower is not deserving of unsecured credit, but is either unwilling or unable to provide a satisfactory margin of collateral value. Examiners should consider senior liens, the costs associated with liquidation of the collateral, and the potential reputation risk that might influence a lender's willingness to liquidate, e.g., lender liability issues.

- Inadequate collateral documentation and valuation — Collateral should be documented by evidence of perfected liens and current appraisals of value. Federal regulations govern the appraisal requirements relating to many forms of real estate lending. Other unregulated types of collateral should also be supported by appraisals or valuations reflecting an economic value commensurate with the loan terms. Loans for which the bank is not materially relying on the operation or sale of the collateral as repayment (i.e., the bank has truly obtained collateral as an "abundance of caution"), should not be included in this category.

- Overly aggressive loan-to-value (LTV) or advance rates — LTV and advance rates should reflect the useful life of the collateral pledged, depreciation rates, vulnerability to obsolescence, and market volatility. Loans-to-cost (LTC) relationships should also be considered, particularly for real estate projects.

- Inadequate guarantor support — Guarantors may serve a variety of purposes in the credit process, including as an "abundance of caution." Therefore, it is important that guarantor support be analyzed in the context of the bank's actual expectations of the guarantor, as well as the guarantor's willingness to support the credit, if called upon to do so. Inadequate guarantor support may result when the bank relies on a guarantor's presumed financial strength, but has not fully analyzed the guarantor's financial information, including contingent liabilities and liquidity. Inadequate guarantor support may also occur when a guarantor, whose support was critical to the original credit decision, is subsequently released from the obligation without other offsetting support.

The repayment of all loans depends, to some degree, on projected future events. For example, repayment depends on the borrower continuing to operate profitably, asset values remaining within a certain range, etc. However, the word "projected," as used in the following four elements, identifies loans whose repayment is predicated on future events that appear to deviate materially from the historical performance of the borrower, trends within the industry, or general economic trends.

- Repayment highly dependent on projected cash flows — This category includes loans whose repayment relies heavily on optimistic increases in sales volumes, or savings from increased productivity or business consolidation. It may also include loans whose projections do not adequately support debt service over the duration of the loan or whose projections rely on an unfunded revolver or other external sources of capital or liquidity. Real estate loans with limited or no pre-leasing or sales should be considered for this category.

- Repayment highly dependent on projected asset values — This category includes loans that are projected to be repaid from the conversion of assets at a value that exceeds current value when the projected appreciation is not well supported. It may also include loans for which the LTV is too thin to weather a decline in value resulting from normal economic cycles.

- Repayment highly dependent on projected equity values — Loans that are predicated on the projected increasing value of the business as a going concern fit this category. These "enterprise value" loans typically have all the business assets, including goodwill and stock of the borrowing entity, pledged as collateral. "Enterprise values" can fluctuate widely, especially during economic downturns.

- Repayment highly dependent on projected refinancing or recapitalization — Loans in this category are made based on the expectation that proceeds from the issuance of new debt or equity will repay the loan. These are not bridge loans pending a closing; rather, the future debt or equity event is uncommitted or has other elements of uncertainty. They may rely on optimistic assumptions about the future direction or performance of debt markets, equity markets, or interest rates.

References

Circulars

BC 127 (rev), "Uniform Agreement on the Classification of Assets and Appraisal of Securities Held by Banks," April 26, 1991

BC 215, "Guidelines for Collateral Evaluation and Classification of Troubled Energy Loans," June 18, 1986

BC 255, "Troubled Loan Workouts and Loans to Borrowers in Troubled Industries," July 30, 1991

EC 223 and EC 223 Supplement 1, "Guidelines for Collateral Evaluation and Classification of Troubled Energy Loans," June 18, 1986 and August 24, 1984

Bulletins

Banking Bulletin 93-35, "Interagency Definition of Special Mention Assets," June 16, 1993

Banking Bulletin 93-50, "Loan Refinancing," September 3, 1993

OCC 96-43, "Credit Derivatives," August 12, 1996

OCC 97-24, "Credit Scoring Models," May 20, 1997

OCC 2000-16, "Model Validation," May 30, 2000

OCC 2000-20, "Uniform Retail Credit Classification and Account Management Policy," June 20, 2000

Advisory Letters

AL 97-8, "Allowance for Loan and Lease Losses," August 6, 1997

Bank Accounting Advisory Series